A Personal Reflection of the Holocaust

D1440890

By Deli Strummer

Edited by Nancy Heneson

Aurich Press, Baltimore
(301) 296-7121

A Personal Reflection of the Holocaust. Copyright © 1988 by Aurich Press. All rights reserved. Printed in the United States of America. No part of this book may be used or reproduced in any manner whatsoever without written permission except in the case of brief quotations embodied in critical articles and reviews. For information address Aurich Press, 1314 Highland Drive, Baltimore, Maryland, 21239

Printed by H.G. Roebuck & Son, Inc.

Library of Congress Catalog Number 88-83595

Copyright © 1988 by Deli Strummer

ISBN 0-9622135-0-0

DEDICATION

This book is dedicated to many of my friends,
who have helped me when I needed it most.

*"It is impossible for us today to imagine what
happened then, but it did happen. And Germany
bears the responsibility for it in history."*

Helmut Kohl,
Chancellor of the
Federal Republic of Germany
Israel, 1984

AN ACKNOWLEDGEMENT

My participation for many years in Holocaust Awareness programs resulted in a fortunate incident—meeting Deli Strummer, a valiant lady who suffered the incomprehensible under the Nazis, survived and was at the death camp, Mauthausen, in Austria, when American troops liberated the inmates on May 5, 1945. I was one of the soldiers who went into this extermination center and was shocked at the horrors that we discovered there. During its existence the number of prisoners exceeded 206,000, of which more than 120,000, including some American servicemen, died. Mauthausen, created by Hitler and Himmler for the alleged enemies of Nazi Germany, was one of the most brutal camps; it had only one purpose—death.

I had avoided returning to that evil place until May 5. 1985, the anniversary marking the liberation of the annihilation camp exactly four decades earlier. At that time the American Broadcasting Company selected and sent me to Mauthausen for an on-site interview with David Hartman, host of the "Good Morning America" program that was televised internationally. When I approached the massive, wooden gate, flanked on each side by high turrets with fortress-like, stone walls encircling the area, a vivid, mental flashback occurred immediately.

v

The first recollection of that fateful day in 1945 was our drawing near to Mauthausen and the startling contrast between the picturesque Austrian landscape and the hideousness that we would witness shortly. Upon reaching the gateway and dismounting from my jeep, I felt a brief chill. Perhaps this was an omen of the inhumanity that we would observe and the countless atrocities that would be described to us by the survivors of this abode of the lost.

After entering, I could hardly believe the sights before me. Bodies were piled throughout the camp. Countless men in striped prisoner attire were wandering around, almost aimlessly. Most were living skeletons, weighing not more than 80 or 90 pounds; the dazed, almost lifeless look in their eyes was unforgettable. I sensed immediately their feeling of constant suffering and current mental confusion, along with the indescribable joy of liberation, yet lacking the ability to express themselves. Some threw their arms around the Americans but many were bewildered, just staring and apparently not fully convinced that they were really freed from their boundless torment.

Many survivors , in addition to severe malnutrition, had typhus fever, typhoid, tuberculosis, pneumonia, dysentery or other severe infections that were rampant throughout the camp. It was distressing to learn subsequently that at least 3,000 died during the next thirty days because of their weakened physical condition.

Living conditions for the inmates were abominable. Three or four men occupied a single bunk and shared a thin blanket. They slept on wooden planks—no mattress—no pillow, and no source of heat in the filthy barracks. The accounts of brutality and methods of killing described by the prisoners seemed almost endless. Survivors led me to places of execution and torture where they had lost relatives and friends. I listened with revulsion to the harrowing narrations of barbarism that had occurred. Prisoners were shoved by SS guards from the precipice of a quarry to jagged rocks about 200 feet below the ledge. Other were shot, gassed, strangled, buried alive, electrocuted, thrown into cement mixers, torn apart by dogs and gnawed to death by rats in a special SS torture technique.

I continued walking, looking and listening, still not fully trusting what I was seeing and hearing, hoping that I was asleep and I would awaken to discover that this was only a horrible nightmare. The episode, however, was not merely a disturbing dream but a gruesome reality.

A few hours later, my comrades and I left this mass-murder site. Although we were combat-hardened infantrymen, accustomed to daily death and destruction, this appalling experience affected us greatly. We knew, then, in 1945, that Mauthausen would remain in our minds and hearts forever.

Deli Strummer courageously endured the pain and grief of Mauthausen and other nefarious places. I am elated that she has completed the extremely difficult task of writing the factual account of her personal involvement in the Holocaust. Only those who have suffered the terrors of that time can describe it adequately and this written work will contribute greatly to the knowledge of that catastrophe. Her story should be beneficial to those, especially our youth, who may have only a limited knowledge of these tragic events. This publication refutes the lies of those who fraudulently claim that the Holocaust is a myth. The heartbreaking happenings described by the author disproves unequivocally that despicable falsehood. The Holocaust must never be forgotten and every effort must be made to prevent it from happening again. This book will be significant in achieving those important objectives.

Colonel (Retired) Edmund F. Murtha

FOREWORD

This is a story of time and place. It chronicles a time of incomprehensible horror; It portrays the places that shaped both the perpetrators and the surviving victims of that time. It also is the story of one person's magnificent spiritual strength, and of hope, forgiveness and restoration in other times, other places.

It is a story of patriotism to two lands: of loyalty to one, betrayed by madness; of profound gratitude to the other, earned by the offer of liberty and peace.

Above all, it is a story of truth. The torment of Deli Strummer must be multiplied by many millions. Millions of human beings who lost their future, who leave no memories.

The fact of the Holocaust must be communicated repeatedly, for without communication, there can be no remembering, there can be no sense of outrage. Without outrage, there is complacency. And complacency is what allows all holocausts to happen.

Remember.

Nancy Heneson
Washington, D.C.
May 1988

PREFACE

It took me only 38 years to write this book. I know that my real inspiration and desire came after I gave a special presentation to eighth-graders and their teachers at the North East Middle School in Baltimore, Maryland in December, 1981.

I spoke of a terrible time in European history—the third and fourth decades of the twentieth century. The topic was my personal involvement in the Holocaust, the name given to the destruction of six million Jews and millions of others under the reign of Adolf Hitler. My audience sat in rapt attention, horrified by my story, living through it with me in one meaningful afternoon.

Afterwards one of the youngsters told me, "You must write a book. You have so much to tell. We take so many things for granted in our country and in our lives."

My young friend, you were right. We, as Americans, must realize what a blessed world we live in, and what the freedoms of democracy mean to those who survived another kind of world, where terrors beyond imagining were commonplace.

CHAPTER ONE

The Vienna I Loved

Sometimes it seems like yesterday that my parents took my sister, Lizi, and me to the playground in Vienna, Austria. I was a proud little girl, blessed with wonderful parents. The fact that my father was a Jew and my mother a non-Jew by birth meant only that we had more holidays to celebrate, more chances to be happy.

Although my mother converted to Judaism the day she married my father (a common occurrence in those days), her parents celebrated the Christian holidays in our home. Both sides of the family joined in all religious celebrations, and that meant lots and lots of relatives congregating at our house: my father's eleven brothers and sisters, aunts, uncles, cousins, and best of all, my four beloved grandparents.

My memories of this time are so vivid. When I was about six years old, I spent many weekends with my Gentile grandmother. She took Lizi and me to a magical thing called the May Procession, where children paraded through the streets of Vienna, handing flowers to everyone they saw. And when confirmation day came for the non-Jewish girls and boys, Lizi and I joined in. The children received religious blessings in a very beautiful city park; Lizi and I drove there in a decorated horse and carriage, complete with balloons. We felt like princesses in a fairy tale.

Vienna was then such a joyous place.

Memories of my Jewish upbringing are just as vivid. On Saturday afternoons I walked to synagogue with my father's parents. The children gave special presentations as part of the service. After we had sung our songs, there was always that special walk down the Hauptallee*, stopping for chocolate candies and Viennese pastry.

*Main Street

1

A Personal Reflection of the Holocaust

Of course, honoring the religions of both sets of grand-parents did cause confusion. At one holiday dinner for 71 relatives, we had gefilte fish for my father's family and baked carp for my mother's. My mother's mother tried so hard to keep the foods separate. Was it a surprise for her when my Aunt Flo tasted my Uncle Fritz's gefilte fish and my Aunt Antony ate some of my grandfather's carp! Such serious problems we had in those days.

My mother was a famous singer in that music-loving city, and my father a successful businessman. In his spare time, he composed music and lyrics. My sister and I had a childhood filled with the love of music and art.

Lizi was a little lady, loved by everyone. She simply could do no wrong. But I was full of vim and mischief, a kid who really loved chocolate... and paid the price! There was the time Mother prepared chocolate balls, a delicious Viennese treat. She stored them away in a high closet in the living room to dry. I walked innocently into the room with my baby carriage. When I came to a particular couch, I climbed up on it, reached into the closet, took a handful of chocolate balls, put them into my carriage, went back behind a curtain, and had a feast. I continued the subterfuge for several days, until my Aunt Flo came for a visit. Mother wanted to proudly present her new dessert, but only one ball was left! One ball I obviously could not reach. I got my punishment, but believe me, it was worth it.

When I was 12 and Lizi was 14, my brother Fritz was born. What a joy to my father. He idolized Fritz. Years later, when Julius was born, it seemed his happiness was complete. But as the 1930's began to unfold, this calm and joyful period in our lives came abruptly to a close.

In the early 1930s, a terrible depression hit Europe. Everyone had to struggle to make ends meet. Along came Hitler, full of promises to improve the lot of the German people. Germany had been hit particularly hard by the depression, and

2

many of her people were ready to accept even the most wicked solutions to their domestic despair.

By 1933, Hitler and his National Socialist (Nazi) Party ruled Germany. The Nazis' anti-Semitic ravings began to drive the Jews out of that country and into Austria, which looked safe.

Indeed, my father and many other men of similar position felt sure that nothing could ever happen to him or his family. But when the first wave of German-Jewish immigrants arrived in Austria in 1933, Austria's Jews grew concerned. Yet many insisted that this Hitler character would never gain a foothold outside of Germany.

How different everything proved to be by 1938. Like a raging infection, Austria-born Hitler spread his power to Austria and through Europe. In that year, our tragedy began. My father, with all his medals of honor from World War I, could not believe that his Austria would desert him. What a cruel awakening it was for him!

One memory remains particularly vivid from that crucial spring day in 1938, the first day of Germany's occupation of Vienna. "God bless Austria!" were the last words we heard on the radio by Chancellor Schusnick. Minutes later the song of the new German government, "Die Fahnen Hoch, die Reihen Fest Geschlossen" (Fly the Flags High, Close the Ranks Tight), blared over the radio in a city that used to hear Strauss' waltzes.

"God help Austria," my mother said.

It took a very short time for the wickedness of the Third Reich (as Hitler's reign was known) to reach our home. The Nazis forced my father to sell his business for a ridiculously low price and to surrender his other possessions. My mother's life turned into another kind of hell. Because she had been born a Christian, the Nazis tried very hard to separate her from my father. How? By torture.

3

A Personal Reflection of the Holocaust

There was a special place in Vienna called Elizabeth Promenade. There was the main office of Hitler's elite guard, or *Schutzstaffel* (SS). My parents were taken there, immediately separated, and tortured. My mother's hands, of which she was so proud, were put in a very tight press. Even this could not make her say, "I leave my husband; I leave my children." When her torturers relieved the press, my mother's fingers were broken and her spirit crushed. As long as I live, I will not forget the look on her face after 24 hours in that place of misery.

What in history can explain such wickedness? Humans destroying humans, systematically, year after year. That was the real horror—that there was a system to this unbelievable degradation.

We had many neighbors; neighbors who were proud of my parents; neighbors who enjoyed the holidays with us; neighbors who were more like family to us than acquaintances; neighbors who escorted the SS as they marched into our home.

My mother kept her jewelry in the linen closet; a "safe" place, according to a European old wive's tale. Gullible and outspoken, she thought nothing of telling the neighbors about her hiding place. They knew so well, they just pointed toward the closet. Moments later everything was gone.

They threw my baby brother Julius from his crib, where they were sure my parents had hidden money. They found nothing. Then they rolled up our beautiful Persian carpets, hoisted them onto their shoulders, and marched out. Our neighbors, the friends of yesterday, now followed the SS.

But they overlooked one thing: the children's piggy bank. When she was certain they were gone, my mother broke off the head of the pig. Out tumbled all the small change we had been saving, enough now to buy a loaf of bread for the evening meal.

How quickly life changed for us all! Every Jewish person in Vienna was swiftly labeled with a Star of David. Whatever we wore, a yellow star had to be pinned to it. Our homes were taken and we were herded together, five families to one apartment. Can you imagine 32 people sleeping in a three-bedroom apartment? Food was scarce. Whatever could be done to humiliate us, was done.

I remembered the years of my early childhood. People were so natural and friendly; hours of conversation about nothing; a discussion in front of a mailbox. Everyone knew everyone else's business. Hikes in the Vienna woods, reunions in the rathskellers*, theater; that was my Vienna before 1938.

I am writing and thinking and wondering, how it is possible that I am here to tell about this terrible unhappiness? I never thought I would be able to speak out about this part of my life, but I know that I must. For there is too much temptation to believe this horror never happened.

Again and again the SS sought out my father and tortured him. They broke him, this old general of the Kaiser's Austrian army. My mother was still the stronger one and decided to leave her home, her beautiful Vienna. My mother convinced my father that the family should immigrate to a better part of the world, "wherever they want us," she said.

We spent three days in front of the American Consulate in Vienna, but it was hopeless. We didn't even get inside the building. There were just too many people and too little time left. Now my father asked himself, "Why didn't I do it earlier? Why didn't I believe?" But he was Austrian, wasn't he? And what real harm could come to a citizen of Austria?

On November 9, 1938: Kristallnacht** in Europe. A seventeen-year-old Jewish boy, Herschel Grynszpan, whose parents were deported from Germany to Poland, assassinated

* Intimate wine bars

** Crystal night—so named for the huge amount of shattered glass from vandalized and destroyed buildings.

Ernest Von Rath, (Third Secretary of the German Embassy in Paris). That night, hundreds and hundreds of Jews were rounded up on the streets. Jewish businesses were destroyed. Synagogues were set aflame, prayer books turned into mountains of ashes. It was the greatest spontaneous outpouring of hatred against the Jews the twentieth century had witnessed.

I saw our synagogue, a fireball against the Vienna sky. I could not understand: it was too much to take in for a child who had spent only golden moments with her grandparents in that temple. Flames and ashes were all I could see, symbols of hate and desire for the destruction of every Jew in Europe. Hitler had wakened a slumbering monster. Once we had felt secure; now there was only fright, bitterness and a paralyzing loss of hope.

In 1938, I was only 16 years old, but because I was a Jew, I was forbidden to continue schooling. Fortunately, I already had enough education to enter a training program for nurses in a Jewish hospital. Even as a little girl, I had been excited by the idea of medicine. Now, I could not consider studying to be a doctor, but I could participate in the life of a hospital as a nurse.

Under the new order, Jews in Austria were strictly segregated. They, therefore, had to create their own hospital out of a former Jewish nursing home that was mostly staffed by old Gentile nurses. Overnight, those nurses became our teachers. Need I say that they were less than kind to their Jewish trainees? Perhaps because they knew that one day we would replace them, they were nasty to us, gave us the worst jobs and made our training hard, disagreeable, and uncomfortable.

In those years of training, I made a young friend who also became a nursing student. Unfortunately, shortly after we met, her mother took severely ill and died of meningitis. This woman had been my patient, and out of a feeling of closeness to her, I promised never to leave her daughter, Nita; to be with her and help her as much as I could. Nita and I became the closest thing to sisters. Together we were to face the tragic years ahead.

In 1940 Nita and I graduated from the training program and became full-fledged nurses. We were enthusiastic, and proud of our new profession. But in those last two years, my parent's lives had become intolerable. My Uncle Siegfried had taken Lizi to Belgium. Now that a war was on amid the Nazis' unrelenting tortures, my parents realized that the only alternative was to hide. Miraculously, a few brave people helped my family go underground.

There was an old farmhouse near my grandfather's former home. The people living there knew my family and courageously agreed to shelter my parents and brothers. With no heat, little food and enough scares to fill a lifetime, they waited. Many times there were knocks outside; soldiers coming to look for people hiding. My family would crawl under the straw, my mother stuffing it into my little brother's mouth to keep him quiet. Together they bore these hardships, and together they survived.

In 1941 the ultimate horror began for Nita and me. They rounded us up right in the hospital, along with many of our ailing patients. We were given an hour to pack and then herded to a "collection point" in Vienna, where other Jews waited to be sent away to God knew where.

Why didn't we fight? I suppose that after years of living in fear and humiliation, we were too tired to care. The daily waiting and daily listening to knocks on the door and noises outside—we felt almost ready for this ordeal.

We travelled by train. Our captors told us we would be killed if we tried to hide any valuables we might still have. Everything of value flew out of the train windows into the grass. Finally they told us our destination: Theresienstadt*, in Czechoslovakia.

* Curently named Terezin

7

CHAPTER TWO

Theresienstadt

Nita and I reached Theresienstadt holding two suitcases each, all that remained of our former lives.

The city was so small that in 15 minutes you could walk from one end to the other. Here, thousands and thousands of people were crowded together. Most of us lived in attics of buildings, with little food and much hard work. The men worked outside, digging ditches and repairing the streets. Nita and I worked under very poor conditions in a hastily assembled hospital. Nita underwent another ordeal: she fell ill and survived serious abdominal surgery on the strength of her youth and her will to live.

All sorts of wicked practices went on in Theresienstadt. We were forced to send cards to whatever family we still had left in Vienna. We were well, the cards said, but we need supplies, as many as you can send. The parcels came, and then the SS confiscated nearly all of them.

I remember the day the Red Cross came to Theresienstadt. Like a miracle, our surroundings suddenly became beautiful. In just a few days, our captors had managed to build us a coffee house and a music pavilion, complete with concerts. They brought in loads of food, good Viennese pastry, anything that harkened back to our former, normal world. Then we learned that the Red Cross was coming.

Up walked the Gauleiter, or camp leader, with members of the Red Cross. He greeted us cordially and asked after our health. I could not believe that the Red Cross could be so completely taken in. Couldn't they tell just by looking at us that we were overworked and starving?

Yet not one protested. And the moment they left the camp, it was as if a building had collapsed in seconds. Everything returned to the sickening state we now thought of as "normal."

I could continue on about Theresienstadt, but I have to realize that it was at least a place where one could expect to survive. If anything, I try to think kindly of Theresienstadt. It was there both Nita and I fell in love. Three months after Nita met Gary and I met Ben, we all decided to marry. I couldn't help thinking of the years before 1938, how my parents talked of the day I would be married, and how elegantly my proud father would have given me away.

Now here we were, exchanging vows under the most terrible circumstances, in worn-out clothing, pieces of metal on our fingers. But we had a Rabbi to give us the blessing, and as he performed that precious ceremony, a shaft of light brightened our crowded attic. I hoped that God had sent this little light for the four of us.

My marriage lasted three months. Yet in those three months, Ben and I made as many plans as couples expecting to spend a lifetime together. We dreamed the same dreams, with no chance of realizing them.

One day, not too long after the Red Cross had come and gone, the order came to our camp for every male to report. The Nazis were opening a new camp and males were to be taken first. Transport began immediately. I don't have to tell you how I felt. Here we were, just starting to know each other, and we knew now that we would be separated, possibly forever. When the news came, I could almost count the hours Ben and I had been together. I know I counted the nights.

Ben and Gary were taken together. After the war, we learned that they had gone to Dachau, a death camp in

9

the suburbs of Munich, Germany. Shortly after they left, Nita and I were taken out of Theresienstadt. It may sound strange, but we were happy to move to a new camp. We were certain then of a reunion with our husbands. We travelled by train for hours and hours, and reached our destination at dawn. We were in Poland. I looked out the train window and there it was...Auschwitz.

CHAPTER THREE

Auschwitz

Many books have been written about the injustice and inhumanity of life in a concentration camp. Yet there are no words powerful enough to describe the hellish, degrading, deathly existence in one of them. The continual torture, destruction of human rights and violation of human dignity left all of us with little faith that we would ever come out alive. Every day created more fear of what tomorrow would bring.

I did not know what to expect on the day of my arrival in Auschwitz. However, I soon discovered that only two possible fates awaited me: to be worked nearly to death and then exterminated, or to be killed right away.

I suppose it could be called good fortune that Nita and I were young and fairly healthy looking. I heard the brutal voices of the people who had been our guards saying, "Heraus, heraus, heraus (get out of the train)!" Then we formed two lines, and two lines were formed by SS guards. They looked into each of our faces and told us, "left," or "right." Left meant hard labor and right meant immediate death. I felt the blood drain from my face. I saw children torn from their parents. Fearful, screaming voices, hands raised up for mercy to the sky.

Nita and I turned left.

I was thrown into a barrack and all my clothes removed. Everything we had brought from Theresienstadt remained on the train. Our heads were shaved, as was every part of the body that had hair. We looked like sheered sheep. The guards gave us one piece of ill-fitting clothing, but nothing for our feet. The temperature outside was near zero.

Then the guards forced us into a chamber with

nozzles on the wall that looked like showerheads. Human bones lay on the floor. We knew where we were. What we didn't know, couldn't know, was our captors' choice. Would those nozzles spray water, or the deadly gas? Waiting, bodies pressed tightly together.... My childhood, my whole life, flashed like lightning before me. I tried to remember the good things; I knew it would be the last time I would remember anything. Then it came...that beautiful moment. Ice-cold water ran down over my body. It felt like heaven, like the best thing that could ever happen. My life had been given back to me.

I went through this experience five times. Five times I was taken into different gas chambers, and five times I was fortunate enough to get away with a mass shower.

After our mass shower, the guards lined us outside. They told us: "You are prisoners of Auschwitz. You have a certain time to live here. We are going to determine how long you will live. You are not anyone with a name anymore. You are a number. You will obey orders and remember there is nobody, nobody ever who will leave Auschwitz alive."

Our sleeping quarters in this hellish place were no better than chicken coops. No blankets, no pillows, no towels or tooth brushes, only the coops housing ten bodies tightly squeezed together.

Food became a luxury. Occasionally, the guards brought us a large pot filled with hot water and something like vegetables swimming around in it. Everyone rushed to the pot and grabbed whatever they could. Imagine being willing to fight almost to the death for one filthy morsel. Auschwitz spared many the gas chamber—it killed them by starving instead.

The need for privacy counted for absolutely nothing in this place. Once a day they took us in rows of 200 to the "latrine," a glorified name for an outside ditch with some wooden planks over it and a few big pots in the middle. If you were at the end of the line, you most likely didn't get your turn until the next time, 12-14 hours later. It was all just another way for our captors to twist a normal activity into the total destruction of human dignity. In those days, that was the name of the game.

Our captors certainly had no passion. It must be remembered that we were all fairly young women and wore practically no clothing most of the time. Yet if the SS ever did see us as women, they couldn't even vent those feelings in a "normal" way. Instead, they played a sadistic game: smoking cigarettes and stubbing them out on our naked skin. Even now, when I look at the burn scars all over my body, I feel anger, frustration and humiliation.

Worse than these burns, is the memory burned into my brain of a particular Sunday afternoon at Auschwitz. I heard a terrific uproar outside the barracks. I tried to see what was happening, found a small hole in the wall, and saw a line-up of children and adults. A whole platoon of SS was having target practice, aiming at the childrens' heads. I saw mothers reaching out for their little ones. I saw them throwing their bodies over their dying children. I heard them pleading, "Please take me. Please don't let me live without my child." It was carnival time for the SS, Sunday afternoon in Auschwitz.

"You are a number. You will never get out of here."

I was assigned to hard labor in an airplane factory. Building airplane parts is very heavy work. With so little food available, we knew we couldn't last too long. Sometimes it would help to drift back, to go to another place inside my mind. I would think about the day the Red Cross came to Theresienstadt. I remembered sitting with my young husband in that hastily built coffee house. Once during the reverie, it came to me: that was the only day in our married life in which we lived like human beings.

In my frustration, I found a piece of lead and some scraps of paper, and I wrote my name. I was caught and accused of trying to smuggle my name out of the camp. For that, they beat me with leather belts filled with steel and iron. I shielded my eyes from the blows—the possibility of losing my sight frightened me the most—and only by the grace of God did they finally walk away, leaving me lying in my own blood.

In Auschwitz, I began to believe that there was nothing and no one in this life with the power to save me. Yet despite all the hunger, torture and humiliation, I never stopped wanting to live. On one hand, the desire to live; on the other, conviction that I would not come out of this terrible time alive. It was like trying to burn a flame in an airless, endless tunnel.

The only way to delay death was not to show our weakness. One time we had to stand for hours in the cold. I felt every bit of life leaving my body. Finally, I fainted. When I came to, I was lying in my face in a puddle of dirty rainwater. Nita and our comrades quickly dragged me to my feet. They knew that if the guards saw me on the ground, they would either shoot me immediately, or torture me to death. Once again, I was saved; once more given back to life.

As we continued to work in the factory, our hair slowly began to grow back. I had a terrible desire for a comb or a knife, something to remind me of civilized life. Though I knew it could mean death if I were caught, I stole pieces of metal from the airplane materials. It took me almost two months to construct something resembling a comb. I also made a knife out of the blade of a saw. How proud we were, Nita, our friends and I! That comb and

14

knife became our talisman.

Now that we had a knife, we could cut and eat the dirty grass as we walked. Sometimes, we were able to fish potato skins from the garbage. We used the knife to divide the skins and ate with the same gusto others reserved for the finest pastry, the sweetest candy.

Somehow Nita and I managed to keep the knife and comb hidden from the SS. During the inspections, we passed them behind us from the hand of one friend to another. These items remain in my possession to this day. Proudly I look at them and proudly I say to myself, "You did well."

There are so many things to tell about that time, that place. Yet how do I find the words? Human skin used for lamp-shades. The Nazis needed no laboratory animals to test their experimental drugs; they had the real stuff—Jews by the dozens. As far as they were concerned, we were a very cheap material.

A final memory from Auschwitz: Right in front of my eyes, the SS take my French comrades to the gas chamber. They know where they are going; they know what the choice will be. They preserve their dignity, humanity and patriotism to the end. The last sounds I hear from them are the proud strains of "La Marseillaise."*

* the French national anthem

CHAPTER FOUR

Mauthausen

As the allies moved closer, the SS decided to transfer us to another camp. By "transfer," of course, I mean on foot.

We marched for 18 days; marched and marched and marched, without shoes, with hardly any water. We traveled mostly by night. By day, we were kept in covered cattle trains, hidden from anyone who might ask questions. Tortured by thirst, people fell into puddles and tried to drink dirty rainwater. The moment they were caught, they were killed. To collapse from exhaustion, to starve or to lose your life over a few filthy rain drops—those were the choices you had on this 18-day march.

On one short stretch of the trip which brought us near a city, they packed several hundred of us into a cattle train. Night fell and the train stopped. Joyfully we realized that Czech freedom-fighters were trying to loosen the sides of the train. By the time the train left Czechoslavakia, they had succeeded. People began escaping; among them some of my friends. My heart and soul felt rejuvenated. I wanted to run away with them, but realized at the same moment that Nita could go no farther. She was too sick and hurt to make it. It took me less than a moment to swing my legs back into the cattle car. I couldn't leave her even though she encouraged me saying, "You are still strong enough. Please save your life." Inexplicably, I could not go. I could not break my promise.

The next morning, when the SS opened the door of our car, they found 12 of us left. They beat us so badly, it was a wonder we were able to make the last part of the walk

16

to Mauthausen, to our new prison. I couldn't know then
that this would not be the worst beating of my life. That
would come later, when I begged the guards at Mauthausen
for a pair of wooden clogs for Nita. It was on 2 May 1945;
my 23rd birthday.

*I can still smell that train: I still see the dying. I can still
recall those few remaining people, beaten half to death,
and myself, dragging the woman I called sister like a sack
of potatoes into this camp: Mauthausen on the Danube, in
Austria. I was back in my own country, and my years of
agony were not over.*

Before 1938, Mauthausen literally had been a
prison, known as "The Alcatraz of Europe" because of the
serious criminals serving life sentences there. This was our
final destination, according to the SS plan.

Again, the gas chambers spewed their poison; again
the ovens burned. Defeat was closing in on the Nazis, and
getting rid of any evidence of the "final solution" (destruction of all Jews in Europe) became the major concern of the
SS. Nothing and no one must remain in the world to show
what really happened.

A camp was quickly erected at Mauthausen and
given the name "Wiener Graben"—Vienna's death hole.

*The German army fought hard up to the final hour. Bombs
fell every day; yet to us it was the sound of music. Even
though we knew we might die in the bombing, we rejoiced
in the thought of taking the SS with us. When the bombs
fell during our death march to Mauthausen, the guards had
hidden under our cattle trains. We told each other: "My
dear, if it really hit, we are going to bury them!" But the*

17

bombs never hit. We were convinced that the Americans knew our location. Every city was bombed, yet the concentration camps and the cattle trains were untouched. If the Americans knew we were there, we reasoned, then there was some chance for our survival. And so we came to love the sound of the bombs, not for the destruction they brought, but for the hope they symbolized.

Mauthausen was completely made of stone, with 250 stairs built by the prisoners. The SS had several hundred German Shepherds, which they starved for days. Then they brought the dogs to the bottom of the stairs, they lined up several hundred camp inmates, formed their own line behind them (some holding still more dogs) and pushed forward, very hard. People rolled down 250 stone steps to the starving dogs below. Several days later, we found a pile of their bones in one large ditch.

The yelling and screaming; human cries for mercy: those sounds will be with me forever. Everytime someone in this wonderful life of mine today asks me, "Have you ever forgiven? Have you ever forgotten?" I answer, "I try to —, but I can never forget." And I never have.

Despite everything I saw and heard, life was still important to me. But like everyone else, I had become dulled to the deaths of so many others. When someone died, it meant a place for someone else to sit down, to stretch an ailing, half-demolished body. There were no tears, no words of sorrow, only a moment of relief.

We were not idle in Mauthausen. The electrified fences that ringed the camp soon became entangled with bodies—the bodies of those who tried to escape, or, out of illness and despair, had thrown themselves against the wires. When the fence was full, the guards turned off the electricity, and whoever was left had to remove the bodies. We dug ditches, and with our last bit of strength, buried our comrades. How I prayed then to overcome. How I prayed for justice.

Mauthausen occupied a beautiful spot in the Austrian mountains. There were houses close by, and people couldn't help but know what went on. All the yelling and screaming for mercy; the smell of burnt human flesh; the flag with the Hakenkreutz (swastika) on the dome of the camp; day and night, SS men standing watch: how could these people ever say they didn't know? They knew. They just didn't care.

Perhaps in their defense, I should say they were too afraid to care. Yet how does one explain the songs and slogans that echoed over the Austrian Alps? "Wenn das Juden Blut vom Messer spritzt, Das ist unser Ziel!" (When Jewish blood flows from the knife, then we are victorious); "Wartet nur, ihr mazes Fresser, bald kommt die Nacht, der langen Messer" (Soon it will be night and the long knife for all you matzoh eaters).

Was this fruit of the same seed that produced Mozart and Beethoven?

So punishing was the hunger at Mauthausen that the thought of food became an obsession. People cooked in their minds all day long. Many of us created the best dishes we could think of and then pretended we ate them. I cooked dumplings, dumplings, and more dumplings, and ate and ate and ate.

Occasionally, we were given a slice of bread. However, there was always a reason the second or third day

19

after for them to take it away—punishment for something that never really happened. Still, I managed to save one slice of bread for many days. I presented it to Nita on her birthday. I have given her other birthday presents since, but none so special as that one.

Perhaps it was my responsibility to Nita that kept me going. I never broke the promise I gave to her dying mother. But above even that was the legacy of my upbringing: a profound belief in God. I did not think of this God in a personal sense, but only as some power greater than myself. And in the most terrifying moments of my life, it was to this one God, this power, that I prayed for deliverance.

CHAPTER FIVE

Liberation

Then came the day we saw bombs flying and buildings burning, and heard terrible shouting from all sides. They drove us out of our barracks and up those nightmarish steps, those steps still laden with deteriorating bodies, some with tortured faces still visible. We knew this was to be our last walk.

The last inhabitants of Wiener Graben were taken to the gas chamber. The day was sunny, and once more my childhood passed before me. I carried Nita, memories of a past that now seemed impossible my only strength. After a couple of hours, I couldn't push to the back anymore. I knew we would be the next ones to enter the chamber. I had seen no one come out, proof that this time there would be no shower.

I tried to talk to Nita and tell her how sorry I was. We would soon be with her mother, I said. I had kept my promise the best way I could.

Then suddenly, the SS men started to run. The door to the gas chamber flew open, sending odor of death into the air. Naked people stumbled out gasping for breath. Screams and shouts broke the peace of the bright, sunny morning in the mountains.

We didn't know what had happened. All we saw were those half-crazed people, storming out of the gas chamber. I heard a tremendous clamor from the main camp where the Gentile Polish prisoners were kept. They yelled over the stone walls to us: "We are free. We are free. We are free!" Nita and I still lay on the floor facing the gas chamber. She was too sick to realize what had happened. I was afraid of being shot if I moved. But little by little, we crawled back to the camp. Again we faced those steps. In what seemed like hours, we made it back to that hole of a

21

place that had housed us for nearly six months.

5 May 1945, the day of liberation! Everybody that was a prisoner, every criminal, managed in no time to get a gun. The brave SS guards just dropped everything and ran. I saw a ranking SS officer take the uniform off of a wounded prisoner and try to hide under it. The rest of the prisoners discovered him. He never escaped.

Soon after Nita and I got back to camp, the Americans found us. I will not forget their frozen, absolutely horror-stricken faces. Seeing us, and recognizing that there was something like human creatures staring back at them.

The first thing the Americans did was turn off the electric wire fences. All the time I had been at Mauthausen, I had fantasized about escaping through a hole in the fence. I put Nita in a corner and squeezed through an opening in the wire. I looked up to the sky and there it was: a white flag, flying high on the dome of the camp. The *Hakenkreutz* was gone. "Oh God, it is true. We are free!"

Still the meaning of liberation did not sink in completely. I managed to crawl up a hill to the mountain home that I had seen from the camp for such a long time. I knocked on the door. It opened, someone saw me and called for help. I spoke to a woman in her own language, our language, and begged her for bread, milk, and clothing. She gave me the food and an old dress.

I was eager to get back to Nita. Weak and still dazed, I crawled back to the camp, careful not to spill that precious bit of milk. I found Nita alive, though almost unconscious. I put her under the cold water pump and washed her. Then, as one feeds a sick animal or an infant, I took the corner of the dress, soaked it in the milk, and squeezed it onto her lips. It took a very long time, but it was the only way to get some nourishment into her. Nita would tell me much later that she has no memory of this. For that I am glad.

As the days went by, the soldiers tried hard to help

us. They felt shame for the way we looked, particularly the women, though we had long ceased to remember our former selves. They gave us their shirts. I hugged the still warm cloth to my desecrated body. They cared! Somebody cared for us. Somebody considered us human beings, made of flesh and blood.

The Americans also gave us food, their own cans, anything they had. They dug ditches for us to bury the remaining dead. There was nothing in their power those soldiers did not do for us.

One of the American soldiers seemed to be searching for someone. Finally he asked me, in very broken Yiddish, whether I knew if there were two people in the camp who spoke English. He told me he was looking for his parents, who had been in Austria when the war broke out. His worried face wrenched my heart, but all I could say was that I wish I were able to help. He continued to look at me, finally taking my arm and saying, "One day you'll be in America, and America will make good on you."

I often think about that young soldier, who, in his own sorrow, gave me encouragement when I needed it so badly. At the time, I saw him as a kind and sensitive man. Now I know he was a prophet.

I have looked for this special young man for thirty years, but have never found him. Or maybe, in another sense, I did find him—in every American who has helped me in my new life, my second life. That young man and the other soldiers who fought for us, gave us much more than their shirts and their food...they gave us back ourselves. My gratitude to America will last as long as my life. I know it may be unfashionable to feel such patriotism, yet I am sure that anyone who reads these lines will understand what America stands for to people like me.

A Personal Reflection of the Holocaust

We remained in Mauthausen for several weeks, occupying some of the SS quarters. Because I spoke German, the Americans asked me to make a count of the camp's Austrian survivors. Out of the thousands who had been in Mauthausen, I now only counted seven women, including Nita and myself.

How odd it must seem to be gladdened by a certificate from the U.S. Army stating that we had been liberated under the most terribly inhuman circumstances. But I was happy— after all those years, to have a document with my name on it. My name was my acceptance back into the human race. I have kept that certificate as a prized possession.

Some of the Nazis were captured by their former prisoners. They threw them into a ditch with their comrades' remains. We walked in silence in rows by this place, looking down at the miserable creatures who pleaded for mercy, the miserable souls who just weeks before had revelled in killing so many of our people in the most inhuman ways.

I stood by the side of the ditch, a piece of brick in my hand. In flashes, I saw the rolling heads of those children in Auschwitz. I smelled the gas chamber. I felt the pain of cigarette burns on my body. I remembered my comrades hanging from the wires of the electric fences, and the smirking faces of the SS.

I started to hurl the brick into the ditch; a moment later, I let it fall to the ground beside me. Not because I was a coward, not because I felt no hatred, but because, in that split second, I had become a human being again. I could not hurt or kill. I hoped my fellow survivors would understand, and that the dead would forgive me. I could not do to those men what they had done to me, and I was glad.

CHAPTER SIX

Vienna, 1945

So many ironies surround my departure from Mauthausen. When Nita and I finally left, it was quite literally on the backs of two criminals who had been serving life sentences for robbery and suspected homicide in "The Alcatraz of Europe."

They carried us out of the death camp as though we were little children, piggy-back style. There was no way to get anywhere except on foot. We set out for the train station, which we thought was only a short distance away. But we had to pass through yet another town in occupied Russian territory. Irony of ironies, the Russians immediately took us captive, believing we were German spies. We spoke no Russian, but our American papers spoke for us and the soldiers let us pass.

The train station was a mass of confusion, a miniature version of the turmoil engulfing most of Europe in 1945. If we had hoped to travel like heroes, to return to a hero's reception, we were soon disillusioned. After three hours of riding on the top of the train, we arrived in Vienna, exhausted and shaken. It was the middle of the night. But the darkness did not conceal the destroyed look of the city, a look that seemed to mirror my inner destruction. Vienna was wounded, badly wounded; the city of my own girlhood was gone. Hitler had left his mark on this once serene and beautiful place.

Yet even in this sad and defeated city, how could we help feeling relieved, even happy? We sang as we walked down the familiar streets.

Nita and I were homeless. Again, our two criminals protected us. We spent the night in one of of their homes. After a joyous reunion with her bank robber husband, the lady of the house offered Nita and me a bed. Tired as we were, neither of us could climb in. We took a blanket and ended up on the floor. We had slept on the floor for so many years, I guess a mattress wasn't our style anymore.

A Personal Reflection of the Holocaust

The next morning we tearfully left our chaperone. They were tears of good-bye, but more than that, tears of fright about our future.

Much later Nita and I learned from the newspaper that our two friends had been recaptured and returned to prison. We told the authorities how the men had helped us, but they answered that nothing could make up for their previous crimes. "And what about the crimes of the SS?" we wanted to ask, "Will they pay too?"

Nita and I continued our journey through Vienna, that demolished city, pride of my father, haven of my childhood. Vienna looked bad, nearly as bad as I did. I almost felt we cried for each other: "Your beautiful world of yesterday, what happened to you? Why didn't your people protect you? The ones who really loved you were forced to desert you, forced in the worst inhuman ways, forced to let you go."

We kept on walking. People stared at us. We must have shocked them.

We passed a beauty salon where the women sat outside drying their hair (the city was still without electricity—an aftermath of the war). When I saw them, something happened inside of me. I walked into the salon, took off the rag that covered my head, and, in a very stern voice, demanded a proper haircut. The beautician looked at me and smiled. That made me even angrier. I kept glaring at him, all my frustration pouring out of me, until his smile turned to a look of fear and then, understanding. He took Nita, too, and sat us down, washed our hair and gave us normal haircuts. I looked in a mirror and said to myself, "Welcome home. Your first step into civilization."

Finally we found what I thought might be the neighborhood where my grandparents had lived. Their building was almost totally destroyed, but I found a door at the back, and through it I heard voices. I knocked. A woman looked through the keyhole and said, "We have no room for beggars here."

26

"I am not a beggar," I said. "I'm looking for my parents, and my grandfather's name was Johann Tuerke. " She opened the door and looked at me with a very unbelieving face. After a few moments, she said, "Are you Deli?" Then she cried.

She was an old lady, a good friend of my grandparents. She had been to our home many times to celebrate all sorts of holidays. She fed us and told me my parents were alive, but that I would have to cross the old Danube to find them. "All the bridges are down," she said, "it's nearly impossible to get there." I thanked her and told her we had already come a long way and a hard way, and I was sure we would find the means to reach my parents.

Impatient to near our goal, we walked faster and faster. We crossed one of the old streets and like a mirage the old synagogue of my childhood appeared before me, half in ashes. I came closer, looked up, and saw part of the ceiling almost intact. There were some of the stars of David in the half-burned paint. My memory drifted back to the days when Lizi and I gazed dreamily at them. Then it was my turn to cry.

Finally we approached the river, and it did look almost impossible to cross. People stood on the bank and told us to forget reaching the other side. They did not realize from where we had come. They did not realize how deep our determination was. This safe and normal world seemed suddenly very immature to us. The word "impossible" had become a challenge, not a defeat. (To this day I challenge the word "impossible." I always remember why.)

Nita and I sat on the bank for a couple of hours, trying to gather our strength. Then we plunged, grasping pieces of floating wood and other debris. Nita was holding on so tightly to me; I realized I must again have enough strength for both of us. I swam on. Now the people on the bank shouted their encouragement: "You'll make it, you'll make it!" And we did.

Now we were almost home. The river current had swept us away from our destination; once again we had to

27

walk. By the time we found my parents' street, dusk had fallen. I found the right building—terribly bombed-out like so many others—but I didn't know which apartment was theirs.

Then, next to the staircase, I noticed a door hanging off its hinges. The next moment I was embracing my mother. I hardly recognized her. When they took me, she had been an attractive woman of 40. Now she looked 80. Broken in body, mind and spirit. My father, too, had cracked. The old general of the Kaiser's army, the business-man who never invested a nickel anywhere but in Austria, the man who never deserted his country. How his country had deserted him!

I looked at my parents and my two younger brothers, scared and undernourished. For the first time since leaving Mauthausen, I felt despair. I couldn't help asking myself, "Why did we live through all that hell? Where will I find the answer?"

My dear mother gazed at me, repeating in a voice choked with tears, "You're alive. You're alive!" Then she said I must be very hungry. I told her the story of cooking dumplings in my imagination. She laughed and produced some flour and sugar given to the family by the Red Cross. On a gasoline burner my mother made those dumplings, the food of my dreams for so many years. Then we all sat down and ate together.

Hitler and his war had stolen my brothers' child-hood. Unlike Lizi and I, Fritz and Julius had hardly any schooling. Fritz became the family provider at age 12, mixing cement for the housing industry. Seven-year old Julius was completely underfed. The first time I saw him, my father's special son, he was no more than a shadow with two big ears.

My brothers were old before their time, with no experience of a normal upbringing. My father's memory, after his capture and torture in 1938, grew steadily poorer; once a powerful man, he never regained his health.

Strangely, it was my broken and bewildered mother who recovered best, perhaps because she never lost her love for Vienna, even when the same people who had cheered her on the stage tortured her on the Elizabeth Promenade.

My mother died in Vienna in 1973. On her grave I saw a beautiful flower arrangement with this inscription: "Our dear beloved Anna. We have never forgotten you.—Members of the Viennese Stadt Theater."

My parents, my brothers, myself—all casualties of this nightmare time in history. We endured and hoped and prayed that Lizi, wherever she was, was doing the same.

CHAPTER SEVEN

Bring Them Home

I started to look for a nursing job immediately after I got home. The Jewish hospital was full of sick people from all over who had come to Vienna seeking shelter. There I found an old professor, a fellow survivor of the death camps.

I looked at him; he looked at me. I said, "I think I am not in very good health." He examined me, told me my ribs were damaged and I was generally in pretty rotten shape. "But what can I do?" I asked. He looked at me again and said, "We need nurses so badly." And there I was.

I started right away, working as hard as I could. Salary did not matter—it was enough just to have food for my family and myself, and for Nita.

One day a man walked into the hospital wearing a uniform of a concentration camp warden. Our kitchen manager introduced us and I refused to shake hands. He looked at me, confused, and I told him plainly, "I don't shake hands with a member of the *Gestapo* (secret police)." He answered with a shockingly hardy laugh. Then he explained that he, Hans Weber, had removed the uniform from a warden killed in Buchenwald, another notorious death camp. After seven years in that place, he had no other clothes to wear. The uniform was Hans Weber's coming-home outfit.

How well I understood. I felt almost ashamed for my misjudgment of a man who would soon become a dear friend.

Hans Weber had been a big businessman before Hitler came to power. He ran a large furniture factory. After the war, he was lucky enough to regain some of his possessions immediately. Hans still had connections with a few garment factories, and he used that influence to get Nita and me some decent things to wear. Hans also found us a place to live. I began to think of him as our personal angel.

Hans and I had more in common than the need for

new clothes. Both of us had lost our spouses when they were taken to different camps; both of us now searched extensively for them. Out of this search we founded an organization called "Bring Them Home." With my duties at the hospital and this very special project, I began to lead a full and busy life.

I was so eager, I couldn't cover enough territory. But even as I searched for others, one name, one man, was constantly on my mind. I deeply believed my husband, Ben, was alive and would come back to me. It was inconceivable to me that I could be here and he could be gone. Then, one day, came the tremendous shock, the inevitable awakening. It was morning and I was on hospital duty:

Hans was coming toward me. There was someone behind him...Gary, Nita's husband! I felt both incredulous and overjoyed at the sight of him. My eyes quickly moved from Gary to the spot behind him, but there was nothing, only empty space. By the time I embraced Gary and looked into his eyes, I didn't have to ask. He just shook his head. I knew then that the number one person in my life, my husband of three months, was not coming back.

That night I sat by a fifth-floor hospital window, looking down and thinking, "Why don't you let go? Why don't you finally let go?" But I felt someone or something above me, speaking to me inside my mind: "You have no right, Deli. God gave you a life and now you have to live up to that. You were saved for something; it's time to find out for what." I thought of the camps, all the tortured moments and my own struggle to survive. I had wanted to live then. How could I think of ending my life now? There was so much to live for.

The next day Gary told me about Ben. They had been taken to Dachau, and the SS had assigned them to hard labor. Eventually both of them tried to escape, but they were caught by the police. They pleaded unsuccessfully to be killed then and there rather than be sent back to Dachau.

31

A Personal Reflection of the Holocaust

When they were returned, each landed in what we called a "Stehbunker," which was really a closet just big enough to stand up in. On the floor were hungry rats. (Even today Gary's legs and feet bear the scars of that terrible torment.) From that time on Gary never saw Ben again.

As the Americans closed in, the SS, anxious to destroy the evidence of their crimes, set fire to the barracks at Dachau. Another inmate was able to release Gary from his burning closet. Ben must have been less fortunate.

I know I will never forget the day Hans brought Gary to the hospital. I see Nita embracing her husband, I relive that heart-stopping moment when I realized he came alone; I feel my world going to ashes. Yet I am glad that it happened to me and not Nita. At least one of us saw our dream come true. When I looked at Gary with his arms around Nita, I knew my duty was done. I had fulfilled my promise to her mother.

For almost a year, Nita, Gary and I never ate any fresh bread. We had such a fear of hunger that we stored a loaf of bread away every day, and always ate only the loaf from the day before.
When I walked down the street, I always looked behind me. I would walk two or three steps and then turn around and see if someone was following me. I had to tell myself over and over that a knock on the door no longer meant disaster.

In 1946 I attended the Nurnberg trials as a witness. For three days I listened to all sorts of excuses, passing crimes down the line, swearing to their innocence. Nobody was ever guilty. Nobody ever knew anything. Those murderers of yesterday, how well they pleaded for their own lives now. It sickened me and I left. I have done my share to repay them, I thought. Just leave the rest to God and the law.

In 1947 my sister found her way back to her birthplace. Here was Lizi, Dad's overprotected daughter, a broken young leftover of a Belgian concentration camp.

She held a child in each arm. I just looked at her and figured she would tell me when she was ready.

Little by little, she told me her story. After travelling for many days, Lizi and Uncle Siegfried reached Belgium. Slogging through ice and snow on bad country roads, they finally found a world they thought would mean freedom for them. Everything went well for about two years. Lizi married a Belgian Jew and was soon the mother of a baby girl.

By the time their second child was on the way, hell had broken loose in Belgium. Hitler's army of occupation marched in and began its mission to search and destroy the Jewish people.

Lizi's husband, Leonard, was among the first to be captured. Left with an infant and pregnant with my nephew, Lizi tried to find work. Though several people befriended her and attempted to help, she was caught on the street and carted away with others in an open truck. Suddenly an air raid began. The SS started to run; Lizi grabbed her chance to escape. She jumped out of the truck and ran home to her daughter. Knowing she had nothing left to lose, she begged her friends to hide her and her child. They took Lizi and the baby Jeanette to a place in the country where she hid in a stable.

That same night, Lizi began an early labor. Her son, Charles, was born prematurely under the most primitive conditions, delivered by a Belgian nun who lived close by. No one thought the baby would live; miraculously, he survived.

But Lizi was neither safe nor free. They found her again working in the fields and that was the beginning of her life in a Belgian hard labor camp.

For a whole year, Lizi knew nothing of her children's fate. When she was captured, they had been left with the people who had given her shelter. I am certain that her motherly love and concern kept her going and allowed her to survive on next to nothing. As she said, "It made me strong. It made me stand up when I fell. It made me go on when I felt I couldn't anymore."

A Personal Reflection of the Holocaust

A day of liberation came for Lizi, too. Barely able to walk, she managed to find her way back to the old hiding place, and to her children, kept alive in hiding for a year by her brave Belgian friends.

After everything we went through, could I consider Lizi and myself blessed? I could. My family, through strength and courage, survived. Can we allow ourselves to forget the millions of others, endowed with the same qualities, who did not?

Soon after Lizi returned, my father died. Our hearts broke, but we felt we were thankful that he lived to see his family reunited after years in their separate hells.

Through "Bring Them Home," we found many children in all sorts of situations. Some of them were in Polish camps, some were still in Theresienstadt. Some of them were in Hungary, kept in various cloisters by Christian brothers and nuns, many of whom suffered equally in concentration camps for their bravery and the convictions of their faith.

Our first task was to find temporary homes for these children. One of the many insidious features of Hitler's plan to annihilate the Jewish people was the complete destruction of the records of every Jew captured. Without documents, we had to work extra hard to discover where, and to whom, if they were still alive, these children belonged.

If we could not find any traces of their former lives, we tried to place the children where there was a chance for a better life. Many if them went to Israel and the United States.

While the children waited for their new homes, my co-workers and I worked hard to rebuild their lives and spirits. It was not enough simply to give them shelter; each child needed personal attention to help clear away the physical and emotional wreckage left in the wake of Hitler's reign.

We organized young people into sports clubs under

the blue and white flag of Israel, hoping that this would restore their lives to some semblance of normality. We reclaimed a cottage in the Alps that had been taken from us during Hitler's time. Some of the older boys worked on restoring it and converting it into a clubhouse. We had help from American and European organizations, which donated food and blankets and encouraged us when we felt frustrated or overwhelmed.

To raise money for our children's camp (how odd to use that word that way), we wrote and produced a play entitled "Yesterday, Today and Tomorrow." Through the play, the children acted out their sorrows and fears, but they also learned that they were once more members of a human society, free to share those feelings with others by performing for the public.

The play ran in various Viennese relocation and emigration centers. Two months later, we had enough money to open a camp with a remodeled clubhouse for 85 children.

We played ball, swam and did calisthenics. In the evening, we held "togetherness talks." It was so important for those children to express their feelings, to learn not to be ashamed of their tears, and not to be frightened. On the Friday evening sabbath, we lit candles and sang songs. Above all, we tried to create an atmosphere that would let them forget the past.

One night in the clubhouse I mentioned to another adult that we were a little short on food. What I really meant was that we needed to pick up more supplies.

One of the boys, then 12 years old, must have heard me talking. The next day, loud squawking and screeching made me drop what I was doing. I looked up and there was Heinz coming down the road holding a live chicken in each hand. He was very proud of himself, saying, "You needed food. Here." I thanked him very much and later took the chickens apologetically back to their disgruntled owner. I could not really blame Heinz. His few years had taught him little more than how to scrounge for his survival.

A Personal Reflection of the Holocaust

About 20 years ago I was walking with a friend on Broadway in New York. A young sailor approached, threw his arms around me and yelled, "Remember me?" At first I wasn't sure and then I saw that little dimple on Heinz's face. My chicken-thief had become an officer in the U.S. Marines. That evening was a time for tears and feelings of great pride.

I needed those children as much as they needed me. This great responsibility gave me the courage to face my own life, heavy with disappointments. The exhaustion was a godsend; I closed my eyes each night thanking Him for bringing me this task.

CHAPTER EIGHT

New Places, Old Memories

My career progressed and I moved to a large clinic, which offered me a position as head nurse. During the time I was mulling over this offer, I prepared a patient for facial surgery. As I shaved him, he made conversation, praising my manner of doing things and asking if I had ever worked for the Red Cross.

He also told me that during the war he had been quite a big man. "What did you do in the war?", I asked him. He said, "Well, I was an architect and I was responsible for some of those barracks in the concentration camps. That was my design." Continuing to shave him as calmly as possible, I answered, "I was a prisoner in those camps you so proudly designed."

I walked away and asked one of my colleagues to finish the job. At that moment my decision became final. There was no place for me anymore in a Viennese hospital. There was no room for people like me anywhere in Vienna.

The next morning I went to the American Consulate and registered as a displaced person for emigration to the United States.

Nita and Gary and their 18-month old son, Paul, had left Vienna for the States in 1949. From the moment they touched American ground, only praise and good words flew back to Vienna. I remember asking them so many times, "What are you doing there?" The answer was always, "Everything is just perfect." They were taking care of a big house and Gary was working as a driver for a big firm.

Exactly one year after Nita and Gary left, I received word that my application to emigrate had been cleared. I was ready to join them in a new world.

We left for America from Bremerhaven in Germany

on an old Army ship, The General Sturgis. Our trip was rough. The Atlantic Ocean in March is a most unquiet one. How wonderful that ship's crew was to us! They knew we came as displaced persons from a very bitter time. Yes, we got seasick, but what did it matter, after what we had gone through? All we really needed were their helping hands and reassuring words.

We arrived in New York Harbor on 15 March1950. I have tried many times since to relive the moment I saw the Statue of Liberty, that special lady. So many people raised their arms to her, their tears flowing in joy, relief and hope. We were in a blessed land, and a world where, once again, the word "tomorrow" had meaning.

"Welcome to America," the statue seemed to say. I felt she spoke directly to me; I felt her arms stretched toward me. In her awesome presence, I saw a new life, and strength to conquer the pain of all my yesterdays.

I thought nothing could top my joy at seeing the Statue of Liberty until I found Nita and Paul waiting for me at the dock. Again, there were tears at our greeting, but of a different kind. For this time we cried not only for the incredible good fortune of being reunited, but also for having regained a future.

Nita and Gary lived on the east side of New York in a large building. Their own apartment consisted of one room and a small kitchen with a bathtub in the middle of the floor. Gary worked as the building's superintendent; Nita scrubbed the hallways; even their little Paul pitched in, collecting garbage. This was their perfect world. I say this without sarcasm, for I remember Nita's embrace and her absolutely sincere welcome "to our wonderful world."

I realized immediately that Nita and Gary could not support another person. Also, I already owed a friend back in Vienna 50 dollars. It was time to start hunting for a job.

One of the doctors from the clinic in Vienna had written a very nice recommendation for me to a doctor in

New York. Luckily, he knew an elderly woman who needed a private nurse. Two days after my arrival, I started working. Since that day I have never stopped.

My first trip to an American supermarket left an indelible impression. What trust, I thought. Everybody can take whatever they want. This was a wonderland, a kind of heaven. You could buy what you wanted quickly and without much talk, a blessing for a new immigrant like me. Though I knew practically no English, into my mind popped the phrase, "Only in America."

My dear old lady lived only a short time. While I was nursing her, I met a former acquaintance of my mother who remembered me as a little girl. She was opening a hotel in the Catskill Mountains and invited me to spend the summer there. She was sure I could find something to do to help prepare for the big season.

We had a marvelous summer, sprucing up that old hotel. On Memorial Day the baker ran off, and suddenly I had an official job. I cabled my mother right away, begging for assistance. With her advice came some good Viennese recipes and a letter asking why, after all this money had been spent on my education, I was working as a baker. I really did well that summer.

It was a totally different experience, a challenge and the only time I have stepped out of my professional background to earn a living. Our cakes became so popular that we opened a coffee shop next to the hotel. What a boost to my still-fragile ego. My English was still very poor, but I could bake a mean cake.

After years of hunger, food held a special fascination for me. My summer friends used to take me to an ice cream parlor down the street from the hotel. The only thing I learned to order was a banana split. I had more banana splits that summer than in my whole life. At the end of the season, I climbed onto a scale. I had gained 50 pounds.

From the day I arrived in America, I have encountered almost nothing but generosity from her people. One such lucky meeting in the Catskills launched my career in medical research.

A young doctor spending the summer in the mountains took an interest in me. "You bake well," he said, "but I have a feeling this is not what you always did all your life." I told him about my nursing and my ambition to work in a medical laboratory. He asked me to call him the moment I got back in New York; he would try to help me get started.

That fall I joined a research team investigating antibiotics, at Brooklyn Jewish Hospital. I also began night school and went to Berlitz twice a week to learn English. I started off with more than my share of a busy life. For my success in keeping up with the schedule, I have two of my best American friends to thank: Hallie and Viv.

Hallie, my American surrogate mother, never failed to cry when I told her stories of my former life. She and Viv gave me a home, but even more important than that, Hallie gave me confidence in myself. She went to school with me, pretended that she wanted to broaden her own knowledge. Actually, she was there to help me keep up in my notes in this illogical and confusing new language, American English.

Hallie was so special; she thought nothing of taking two years out of her life to help me. That would have been sacrifice enough, but at the time Hallie was also battling a serious case of psoriasis. She was often very uncomfortable, tortured by a steady pain and excruciating itch, but blessed with an unbelievably sharp sense of humor and a passion to help others. An angel must have watched over me and guided me Hallie's way.

Hallie's efforts and my long nights of studying paid off when I received my certificate of qualification as a

medical laboratory technician. I had had some laboratory
experience my last year in Vienna, and technical things
came easy to me. But, oh, the language barrier! The
Viennese child who had breezed through French and Latin
grew up to find herself in a real struggle with English.

One day I sent my Spanish (another complication!)
assistant out for guinea pigs. In my backward way, I told
him to bring me back some "skinny pigs." He looked at me
uncomprehendingly. I was getting impatient: "Hurry up.
They might close before you get there." The poor man
couldn't help himself. He walked straight to the chiefs
office and asked him, "Where can I get skinny pigs for Deli
this time of day?" The next day I found a note on my lab
table: "Hi, Deli. Skinny pigs are guinea pigs. You got it?"

I found myself in these silly situations time and
time again. It was embarrassing, frustrating, yet in the end
I learned to laugh with my colleagues over my mistakes.
What do you do when you can't find the "who-sis" and
"whatchamacallit" in the dictionary? You call Hallie, who
tells you, "Deli, they mean everything." Then you laugh.
Or when the delivery boy sternly tells you he is unaware of
the store having "new rules." Finally, you figure out the
word you want is "rolls." Then you laugh.

I won't even go into my problems with "he" and
"she." Suffice to say that Berlitz eventually took effect,
and my vocabulary broadened.

*From the moment I made my first nickel in America, I tried
to help my mother back in Austria. She was lonely for me.
Her letters were like conversation; when I read them I often
felt I was sitting right in front of her, facing her, in that old
chair, listening to her dear voice. Though she understood
my wanting to live so far away from the sight of so much
grief and pain, she never really accepted it. I can still see
her face as I prepared to board the ship, still feeling her
arms tightly around me. I hear her say, in a very soft*

41

*voice, "Don't forget us." My littlest brother, Julius, asked
me, "How much does it cost to come to America?" I thought
this was his way of saying "So long." Lizi could not control
her tears. Yes, it was very hard to leave them. But I knew I
had to go. Vienna, the pride and the joy of my childhood,
was full of former sympathizers with the Third Reich. I
wanted to aid the progress of medicine, but I could not
touch those people anymore.*

After eight years at Brooklyn Jewish Hospital in
antibiotics research, I changed my field. I was fortunate to
find a position at Memorial Hospital in Manhattan, which
had a strong affiliation with Sloan-Kettering Institution*, a
true medical research institution. There I developed a good
background in hematology (the study of blood) and was
technically involved in a publication by Dr. Daniel Miller in
the <u>Journal of Hematology</u> of May 1961.

My work at Memorial was interesting. I truly felt I
was in the land of opportunity. I worked hard and I accom-
plished a lot. My achievements were like fragile plants: they
needed constant care at the beginning, but eventually they
yielded the flower of satisfaction. Willingness to work,
initiative, giving of oneself, bettering oneself—I saw these
things as the ideals of American life. And for me, at least,
the ideal became reality.

Eleven years passed before I returned to Vienna to
see my family. My brother Fritz had married. Lizi's happiness came from her children: Charles had grown up to
inherit mother's voice, and had started to study the theater.
Jeanette was her mother's continuing joy. My baby brother
Julius was still very slender; he tried so hard to be the big
man! The most precious part of being home was talking to
my mother. "I thought I would never see you again," she

* now Sloan-Kettering MemorialHospital

said when she first saw me. She hugged me tightly. I felt eleven years of waiting in that one hug.

By 1961 Vienna had repaired much of herself. Still there were reminders of the war and of Hitler's vile achievements. The Opera House still had visible damage and was closed to the public. The old Stefan, one of Vienna's grandest churches, had been nearly destroyed by fire. A young priest now was laboring to save it.

Reminders of the Third Reich seemed to cling to the city. I walked through the old park and gazing at a bench, I saw in my mind's eye: *Für Juden Verboten* (No Jews Allowed). Memories struck like lighting.

For the next week, I tried to enjoy some of the old country, some of its remaining beauty, but I felt empty. I could hardly face the Viennese people, my countrymen of yesterday. Then, as the week neared its end, I realized I was glad. I did not blame the old benches in the park. The old buildings still looked beautiful to me. I still could love the city where I was born and raised, if not all its people. I took long walks with my mother and proudly she introduced me to some of her elderly friends. Still gifted with a sense of humor, she said, "Meet my daughter, the American ambassador." I told her often of my feelings for my new country, my new home: "I wish I could make it yours, Ma." But I knew that if I were to see her again, I would be the one to do the traveling, back to Vienna, my old home.

It would be another five years before I visited Europe again. This time some American friends joined me. I took them to see Mauthausen. Being made of stone, it could not be destroyed. It is kept as a memorial for all victims of the Holocaust. Many nations have placed remembrances there. One of the more powerful ones is the Jewish memorial to six million dead. "Never forget" is the inscription. There is also a plaque for 34 Americans and thousands of photographs, from babies to the elderly, covering the stone walls.

A Personal Reflection of the Holocaust

It wasn't easy for me to go there, but I was determined to show the place to my American friends. We first went there toward dusk. I found my way through the big stone archway, opened the door, and spotted a German Shepherd. I closed the door and ran.

My friends ran after me. They caught up with me and breathlessly I explained what I had seen. The next day I returned in daylight. Very slowly, I opened the same door, and there he was again. A mid-sized dog wagged his tail in friendly greeting. I knew then that the past was past. The stone walls that were once our prison are now protectors of the memory of our irredeemable loss.

The gas ovens at Mauthausen have been preserved. I showed my friends how close Nita and I had come to extermination. I relived with them those horrible moments of seeing half-dead bodies spilling out of the gas chambers. I pointed out the ditches that held thousands of human bones. I wanted them to see and take this memory back to their blessed land. I wanted them to realize what happened here.

Standing among all the reminders, I asked my friends, "How much did Americans know of this?" I looked into their eyes and needed no answer. The Nazis were adept at covering up what they did not want the world to know. How well I remembered the Red Cross in Theresienstadt. I did not feel completely secure until I was home again, in America.

In 1973 I hurried back to Vienna in time to find my mother closing her eyes for the last time. She had often said she wanted to visit me, but her health had grown worse with each passing year. I wonder, though, if she would have come under other circumstances. Her heart and soul were in Vienna; she lived and died a Viennese. She had given her all to that city, and to us.

CHAPTER NINE

Work, Love, Forgiveness

I spent close to six years in cancer research at New York's Memorial Hospital. I came in contact with so many very ailing patients, so many leukemic children. My heart went out to them, and I was proud to be part of Memorial's team effort against the disease. But I was beginning to feel the need to move on.

I learned of a fairly new hospital in Baltimore that had recently opened a research center. Friends who lived down there sent me a newspaper clipping advertising for a position in obstetrical research with special emphasis on the problems of the unborn child.

I thought about this opportunity for days. It seemed so alive, so exciting and refreshing. I sent my resume to Dr. David Turner, who was, in 1962, a leading authority at Sinai Hospital in Baltimore. Two months later, after a lot of anxious waiting and an interview in which I'm sure the pounding of my heart drowned out my voice, I opened the doors to my new laboratory.

I had never been so excited and eager to learn. And learn I did, from one of the brightest, most special and devoted men I have ever known: Dr Joseph Seitschek, then Sinai's chief of obstetrics and gynecology.

The first day I met Dr. Seitschek, he had just arrived from Philadephia to accept his position at Sinai. There we were in the laboratory—he was carrying a distiller and I was holding a flask. He fixed his captivating smile on me and said, "Well, what do you think we should do now?" He had a charming way of putting people at ease. His goals were clear and his interest deep. He was absolutely committed to our work—the development and refinement of liquid chromotography for the analysis of hormones. Sinai became a training center for this new method, which involves the fine separation of molecules for in-depth analysis of biochemical substances.

Over twenty years have passed since that first meeting. Our research division grew from two to seven laboratories. We were capable of doing any hormone assay possible with the use of complex medical technology. A brilliant chemist headed our team. Since Dr. Seitschek, three chairmen of the department had given us their know-how, their ideas their experience and their wisdom.

I had learned so much in all those years. And I was still learning. I had endless curiosity about the unknown and the drive of a perfectionist in my work. How can I ever express my gratitude for the opportunity to have grown in this direction? The demolished, humiliated, nameless being of 40 years ago had become a proud and respected member of an active, expanding medical research team. A childhood dream, shattered and seemingly lost forever, had come true in another time, another place.

I thank and remember the many friends who gave confidence and encouraged me to be the way I am today. I am lucky enough to live in my own house and even luckier to share that home with my dear friend, Maude. Maude is every good thing about America to me: proud, straightforward, big-hearted.

Both of us are extremely fond of dogs. An important member of our household is our little dog Tinker. Tinker is especially loved, having come to fill the void left by the death of our 13-year-old Shu Shu.

Hallie died in 1976. I was with her at the time. She had undergone serious surgery, and we thought then that we would lose her, but she recovered and came to stay with me in Baltimore. Again she fell very ill and entered Sinai Hospital. We tried to help her, to save her life. I spent nights with her, watching her in her restless sleep, asking myself, "Why can't I help her? Where can I find the wisdom and knowledge to make her well?" I suppose God has the answer. He needed an angel and I know he got the best. In my memory and in my heart, Hallie lives on.

Dear Viv has remained one of my best friends. I know we can rely on each other even if we live in different American cities. A bond of almost 30 years of understanding and friendship keeps us together.

In the '60s I met the Washburn family. They owned a 320-acre farm near a small town in Pennsylvania. I spent many vacations there with Doris, a school teacher in Baltimore, and her brother, Wayne, a genuine, hard-working farmer. Again in another time and place, I was able to recapture the family feeling that had been denied me because I happened to be a Jew in Europe in 1938.

My sixtieth birthday was unforgettable. So many of my friends came to honor me. I was full of gratitude for their part in helping me mark a milestone in my life. In the reflective mood that birthdays bring out, I remembered that American soldier in Mauthausen, the one I searched for and never found. Looking at all my friends, I told them I had found the meaning of his words, "America will make good on you." And I realized, that, in these loving people, I *had* rediscovered my American soldier, many times over.

I have received hundreds of letters from young people in schools where I was invited to talk about my experiences in the Holocaust. Here are excerpts from a few of them:

> *"When you went to those concentration camps, did you ever think of suicide? When you were answering my questions, my heart was beating faster than normal. You made me feel, out of 190, that I was the only one in the room. I think our parents should be allowed to come and hear you speak."*

"When you started talking, I could feel the horror and pain and humiliation. I realized how blessed we are in America."

"I know that it was kind of hard bringing out your nightmares of that time, but at least we know now what the Holocaust really was. You were right; violence does not settle anything. I will never forget what you said about everything."

"Now, after I heard your story, I realize that the Holocaust was real. You can see so many pictures and hear so many stories, but it is unbelievable until you met a person who lived through it."

I am sure my readers realize that I am not a professional writer. I am simply a reborn human being, telling my story in a world where I know I am understood. The fears of yesterday revisit me only once in a while in a nightmare—I have truly learned to enjoy the good and normal things in life again. My home is my pride and joy. I love the outdoors and I love animals, particularly dogs. I enjoy cooking, baking (of course!), music and the theater. I believe in physical fitness and swim three-quarters of a mile every day. Clothing and appearance are very important to me. No wonder, considering the way I was forced to look for so long a time.

Above all, I love to entertain my friends. I am happiest when I see them all together having a really good time. Recently, Maude and I bought a second-hand piano for the club room. Now, at parties, my friend Kathy plays away, which adds all the more to the general merriment.

But the real highlight of my party-giving, year after year, is our Fourth of July celebration. All of my friends gather in our big back yard. It is a time to celebrate both independence and togetherness, a time to remember the horror behind the Nazi flag and the hope symbolized by this other flag, flying proudly over my home.

America continues to be good to me in the 1980s. After my retirement as a Medical Researcher at Sinai Hospital in 1987, I continue to bring a message of hope for a peaceful world to people of all ages, especially to young people. I, under the auspices of the Community College of Baltimore and the Baltimore Jewish Council, speak to community organizations and school groups about the Holocaust—to see that this terrible event of the Twentieth Century will never happen again.

In 1988 I began a new venture. I volunteered at the Capital Children's Museum in Washington, D.C., where I am an Eyewitness for the exhibit, "Remember The Children." This exhibit vividly shows the one million five hundred thousand Jewish children who were forcibly removed from normal lives into the horror of the Holocaust. I, as an Eyewitness, narrate the story of this terrible time, keyed to childrens' understanding.

I also maintain my ties with Sinai Hospital by being a Grief Recovery Group Facilitator with their Widowed Persons Service. Knowing how people hurt after loss, I wanted to be trained to give direct service to men and women who have lost a spouse to death. Forging a second career, I now work with small groups of bereaved persons, helping them to realize that there *is* hope.

In never forgetting the pain of yesterday, I go ahead with my life, always with hope. To readers of this book, I bring you the strength of one person—myself—to show you how precious life really is.

I would like to end this book, the story of my life, by reassuring my readers of one important thing: I am most at peace. I will never forget; I have tried to forgive. I have learned that only through forgiveness can you live in peace. With open eyes, I pray for this country, for our children and for their children to come. I have written so much about the bitter years...I will end with the happiest and most meaningful day of my life, 7 December1956.

On that day I became a citizen of the United States. I thank this nation of liberty and freedom for giving me back my life, this time to do more than survive. This time, to live.

EPILOGUE

My sister Lizi and her children, Charles and Jeanette, are still living in Vienna.

Charles was blessed with my mother's musical talent and is active in the theater. He has two sons, Wolfgang and Harold.

Jeanette and her husband, Jishu, are happy and living a good life.

My brother Fritz and his wife Liesel are also in Vienna. They have a lovely teenage daughter, Regina.

My brother Julius and his son Rudi operate a tobacco shop in Vienna. Their scars have healed, as scars do with time. The nightmares and memories still return but all in all they are content and thankful they now can lead a normal life in peace.

My friend, Hans Weber, is also living in Vienna. Ben's whereabouts are unknown. Gary and Nita and their son, Paul, live in New York City.

Both sets of grandparents died of natural causes. Uncle Siegfried was killed in Belgium, and all of my other Jewish relatives, except an aunt in Uruguay and two cousins in Israel, lost their lives in the concentration camps.

A Personal Reflection of the Holocaust